Daughters of the King

PATIENTLY WAITING FOR MARRIAGE
30-DAY DAILY DEVOTIONAL

By Keyle Stateman

Copyright © 2024 by Keyle Stateman

All rights reserved. No part of this publication may be reproduced, distributed or transmitted in any form or by any means, including photocopying, recording, or other electronic or mechanical methods, without the prior written permission of the publisher, except in the case of brief quotations embodied in critical reviews and certain other noncommercial uses permitted by copyright law. For mission requests, write to the publisher, addressed " Attention: Permissions Coordinator," at the address below.

Keyle Stateman/Rejoice Essential Publishing
PO BOX 512
Effingham, SC 29541
www.republishing.org

Unless otherwise indicated, scripture is taken from the King James Version.

Scripture quotations marked (NIV) are taken from the Holy Bible, New International Version®, NIV®. Copyright © 1973, 1978, 1984,

2011 by Biblica, Inc.™ Used by permission of Zondervan. All rights reserved worldwide. www.zondervan.comThe "NIV" and "New International Version" are trademarks registered in the United States Patent and Trademark Office by Biblica, Inc.™

Scripture taken from the New King James Version®. Copyright © 1982 by Thomas Nelson. Used by permission. All rights reserved.

Daughters of the King/Keyle Stateman

ISBN-13: 979-8-3482-0079-4

Dedication

I DEDICATE THIS DEVOTIONAL TO the single woman Of God awaiting God's timing for marriage; remember that you serve an on-time God whose timing is perfect.

Proverbs 31:25 (NIV)

She is clothed with strength and dignity; she can laugh at the days to come.

Table of Contents

DAY 1 1
DAY 2 3
DAY 3 5
DAY 4 7
DAY 5 9
DAY 6 11
DAY 7 13
DAY 8 14
DAY 9 16
DAY 10 18
DAY 11 20
DAY 12 22
DAY 13 24
DAY 14 26
DAY 15 28
DAY 16 30
DAY 17 32
DAY 18 34
DAY 19 36
DAY 20 38
DAY 21 40
DAY 22 42
DAY 23 44

DAY 24	46
DAY 25	48
DAY 26	50
DAY 27	51
DAY 28	53
DAY 29	55
DAY 30	57
ABOUT THE AUTHOR	60

DAY 1

What Is Impossible For Man, Is Possible For God

Luke 1:37 (NKJ)
For nothing will be impossible with God.

I know right now you may feel like there are no prospects in sight that you can see, you may even feel like men don't even notice you when you are out and about. I hope you know that you serve a God of suddenlies, thus be in expectation for God to move on your behalf.

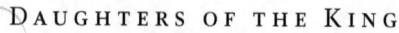

PRAYER

Father, in the name of Jesus, I ask that you open doors of kingdom marriages for my sisters in Christ. What they may feel is far-fetched or even impossible is possible with you Father, for you are the God of suddenlies and nothing is impossible for you God. Lord, I ask that you give my sisters peace as they wait in expectancy for you to move on their behalf. Amen.

DAY 2

Allow God To Order Your Steps

PROVERBS 16:9 (NIV)
In their hearts, humans plan their course, but the Lord establishes their steps.

You may have set a personal goal to be married and have children by a certain age, and that age may have come and gone by now. We must realize that God's thoughts are not our thoughts and His ways are not ours.

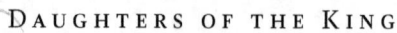
DAUGHTERS OF THE KING

PRAYER

Lord, We thank you that your ways are better than ours. We thank you that we don't have to worry about who, when, and where when it comes to you joining us with our kingdom spouse. We are grateful that our steps are ordered and ordained by you God. We thank you, for you have an appointed time for your daughters to marry in Jesus's name. Amen.

DAY 3

You Will Not Have To Compromise

PROVERBS 10:22 (NKJ)
The blessing of the Lord makes one rich, and adds no sorrow with it.

God's plan for you doesn't require compromising your values or beliefs. Instead, His blessings yield abundance And peace.

PRAYER

Lord, I offer heartfelt thanks for the courage to stand firm in my beliefs and values, while trusting your plan for marriage. Your word says that your blessings makes one rich and adds no sorrow. I'm forever grateful for your love and abundant blessing in my life. Amen.

DAY 4

Don't Be Doubtful While Waiting

JAMES 1:6 (NIV)
But when you ask, you must believe and not doubt, because the one who doubts is like a wave of the sea, blown and tossed by the wind.

It's easy to become doubtful when it seems like everyone else is being blessed with their kingdom spouse except you. You must not let doubt overtake you but instead, stand firm in your faith and trust God.

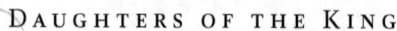

PRAYER

Heavenly Father, Forgive us for any doubt that may enter our minds. Lord, bless your daughters with strength and wisdom and fill them with hope as they wait on you to bless them with the one you have for them in Jesus' name I pray, Amen.

DAY 5

Fear Not!

PSALM 34:4 (NIV) I sought the Lord and he answered me. He delivered me from all my fears.

You can't let fear take hold of you as you wait on the Lord; no matter how long or short your journey to marriage is, you must seek the Lord with any concerns you may have. You must seek the Lord by reading His word, worshiping Him, fasting, and praying.

<u>PRAYER</u>

Heavenly Father, in the name of Jesus. I ask that you remove any fear that your daughters may be experiencing concerning their future. I pray that they will seek you, Lord, for the blueprint concerning their lives. I decree and I declare that your daughters will trust you wholeheartedly God because you know all and you see all In Jesus' name I pray Amen.

DAY 6

Unwavering Faith

HEBREW 10:23 (NIV) LET us hold to the hope we profess, for he who promised is faithful.

No matter what it looks like or feels like in the natural, you have to have unwavering faith that God will bless you with your God-ordained husband in due time.

PRAYER

Lord, Bless your daughters with unwavering faith and wisdom as they trust in you, for your divine plan to unfold in their lives, bless them with the strength to live by faith and not by sight in Jesus' name I pray Amen.

DAY 7

Patience Is Key

ROMANS 8:25 (NIV) But if we hope for what we do not yet have, we wait for it patiently.

Patience purifies your faith, and patiently waiting on God also builds your spiritual endurance as you wait on God to unite you with your kingdom spouse.

PRAYER

Father, bless your daughter with patience as she waits on you to bring forth her kingdom spouse, give her peace and the strength to endure the wait, in Jesus' name I pray. Amen.

DAY 8

Maintain A Posture Hope

PSALM 130:5 (NKJ)
I wait for the Lord, my soul waits, and in His word I do hope.

As you wait on the Lord for marriage, be aware of your attitude and heart posture: are you waiting in despair? Wait with a heart full of expectation, trusting God's plan for your life.

PRAYER

Lord, fill your daughter with hope as she puts her trust, faith, and hope in you; help her to trust your sovereignty, knowing that you work all things for the good of those who love you. Amen.

DAY 9

Don't Get Ahead Of God

LAMENTATIONS 3:25 (NIV)
The Lord is good to those who wait for Him, to the one who seeks him.

Sometimes, it may feel as if God has forgotten about you during your season of waiting as you rejoice with others who are engaged or newly married, but that is far from the truth. God is always close by as you seek His face. Remember, no time is ever wasted as you wait on God. His timing is perfect and His plans for your life are bigger than you can comprehend. Allow God to blow your mind.

PRAYER

Father, Thank you for always remaining faithful to your daughter. Lord your word says you are good to those who wait on you; thus I thank you in advance for the good and perfect gifts you have in store for your daughter. Amen.

DAY 10

God's Blueprint For Your Life Is Filled With Promise And Purpose

JEREMIAH 29:11 (NIV)
For I know the plans I have for you, declares the Lord, plans to prosper you and not to harm you, plans to give you hope and a further.

Even in this mist of your single or waiting season, God has great plans for your future. God is all knowing and has control over your future.

Remember, God's plans are for good, not evil. God desires to prosper and bless His daughters.

PRAYER

Father God, I thank you for the promise in Jeremiah 29:11, reminding your daughter of your sovereign plans for her life. Fill her with hope as you order her steps according to your word in Jesus' name I pray, Amen.

DAY 11

Pray In Faith

MARK 11:24 (NIV)
Therefore I tell you, whatever you ask for In prayer, believe that you have received it, and it will be yours.

Effective prayer requires unwavering faith. One must trust in God's capabilities and intentions without doubting His ability to intervene in your life.

PRAYER

-

Heavenly Father, I come before you with unwavering faith, grounded in your unshakeable goodness. Your word says whatever I ask in prayer, if I believe then I shall receive. Lord, I thank you in advance for answering my prayer. Amen.

DAY 12

God's Timing, Not Mines

PROVERBS 16:9 (KNJ)
A man's heart plans his way but the Lord directs his steps.

We sometimes set specific timelines for key events, such as marriage or starting a family. When those timelines are not met, feelings of inadequacy may emerge; that is a trick of the enemy. It's crucial to remember that God orchestrates your life's journey.

PRAYER

Lord, guide your daughter in your divine timing. Bless her with wisdom to trust your plans.

God's Timing, Not Mines

When her expectations differ from yours, help her to surrender to your will. May her heart find rest in your goodness and her life reflects your glory. Amen.

DAY 13

Trust The One Who Holds Your Future

PROVERBS 3:5-6 (NIV)
Trust in the Lord with all your heart and lean not on your own understanding. In all your ways submit to him and he will make your paths straight.

Sometimes, we are uncertain of our future. However God is not. He knows all and sees all. Wholeheartedly trust him without reservation, allowing God to guide you in His ways and make your paths straight.

PRAYER

Lord, I trust you with all my heart. Help me to surrender my understanding, grant me wisdom to discern your will and the courage to follow your lead. Thank you for your faithfulness and love, in Jesus' name, I pray Amen.

DAY 14

Finding Peace In The Wait

PHILIPPIANS 4:6-8 (NIV)
Do not be anxious about anything, but in every situation, by prayer and petition, with thanksgiving, present your request to God.

And the peace of God, which transcends all understanding, will guard your hearts and your minds in Christ Jesus. You don't have to live your life in fear and worry. Instead, pray and give God thanks in all situations, and watch God give you peace beyond belief and understanding.

PRAYER

Lord, I thank you that I will pray about everything instead of worrying. I thank you that I can find peace in your presence and in your promises. I thank you in advance for answering my prayers in Jesus' name, I pray Amen.

DAY 15

Rise And Pray!

PSALM 5:3 (NIV)
In the morning, Lord, you hear my voice, in the morning I lay my request before you and wait expectantly.

Begin each day by approaching God's throne, knowing that He is deeply aware of every aspect of your life, from your name to the number of hairs on your head. As His daughter, you have access to His attentive ear. Bring your prayer request before Him with faith and anticipation.

<u>PRAYER</u>

Lord, I gratefully come before your throne, bringing my morning prayer request before you. Guide my thoughts and prayers today. Help me to trust in your divine sovereignty, in Jesus' name I pray Amen.

DAY 16

Resist Compromise

ROMANS 8:25 (NIV)
But if we hope for what we do not yet have, we wait for it patiently.

Don't settle for a wolf in sheep's clothing. Do not allow deception from the enemy to manipulate you into thinking your wait is in vain, causing you to miss out on the one your Father has ordained for you.

PRAYER

Lord, bless me with patience and wisdom as I wait for you to fulfill your promises in my life.

Help me to wait in expectation and faith, knowing that you are working everything out on my behalf. Amen.

DAY 17

Tired And Weary From The Wait

ISAIAH 40:31 (KJV)
But they that wait upon the Lord shall renew their strength, they shall mount up with wings as eagles, they shall run, and not be weary, and they shall walk, and not faint.

In the stillness of waiting, find strength in God's promise to renew and restore you, release your doubts, and trust His timing is perfect. Allow God to transform your season of waiting into a season of spiritual growth and empowerment.

PRAYER

Heavenly Father, Help me to wait on you and trust in your unfailing love. Renew my hope and strength so that I may soar like eagles. Bless me with the courage to wait on you with endurance and I thank you for being my supernatural strength and joy, Amen.

DAY 18

You Are Never Alone

DEUTERONOMY 31:8 (NIV)
The Lord himself goes before you and will be with you, he will never leave you nor forsake you. Do not be afraid, do not be discouraged.

No matter how lonely you may feel at times, know that your Heavenly Father is ALWAYS with you. He goes before you and makes your crooked paths straight. God will never leave you. Remember, His love is unconditional and He is a covenant-keeping God.

You Are Never Alone

PRAYER

Lord, I thank you that I am never alone. When loneliness and fear try to creep in, help me to remember your faithfulness. Thank you for always holding me close and being my comfort. May your presence fill me with peace and confidence. Amen.

DAY 19

The Desires Of Your Heart

PSALMS 37:4 (NIV)
Take delight in the Lord and he will give you the desires of your heart.

The word delight means to experience great pleasure, satisfaction, or happiness. This is experienced when you take delight in the Lord. When you prioritize your relationship with God, He will fulfill the desires of your heart.

Prayer

Lord, I surrender my desires to you, asking that your perfect will be done in my life. Help me to delight in your presence and prioritize our relationship. Bless me with wisdom to understand your plans and purpose for my life, in Jesus' name, I pray Amen.

DAY 20

The Power Of Faith

HEBREWS 11:1 (NIV)
Now faith is confidence in what we hope for and assurance about what we do not see.

You can not waver in your faith when waiting on God. Regardless of your single relationship status, you must understand that you serve a God of sudden transformations and all things are possible with God if you believe and trust in Him.

PRAYER

Lord, I thank you for the gift of faith. Help me to trust in your divine plans and promises for my life even if they appear different in the natural right now. Grant me the confidence in what I hope for and the assurance about what I don't see. Lord, increase my trust in your goodness, love, and sovereignty, in Jesus' mighty name I pray, Amen.

DAY 21

Wait With Hope And Not Despair

ROMANS 15:13 (NIV)
May the God of hope fill you with all joy and peace as you trust in him, so that you may overflow with hope by the power of the Holy Spirit.

Embrace your season of singleness with joy, peace, and purpose as you allow the Holy Spirit to prepare you for God's divine plan as you trust your Father.

PRAYER

Heavenly Father, I thank you for being the God of hope. I ask that you fill me with joy and peace as I trust you. Pour out your Holy Spirit, filling me with overflowing hope in Jesus' name I pray, Amen.

DAY 22

You Are Special

PSALM 139:14(NKJ)
I will praise you, for I am fearfully and wonderfully made, marvelous are your works, and that my soul knows very well.

Don't fall for the deception that your appearance is less than stunning. Your Father created you with care and attention. Every aspect of you was intentionally crafted. You are God's handiwork.

PRAYER

Lord, I praise you because you have fearfully and wonderfully made me. Your works are wonderful, and I know that very well. Help me to recognize my worth in you and appreciate my uniqueness. May your love and acceptance define my self-worth in Jesus' mighty name, I pray, Amen.

DAY 23

God's Appointed Time

ECCLESIASTES 3:1 (KJV)
To everything there is a season, and a time to every purpose under the Heaven.

Don't lose faith during your waiting season. It's natural to wonder if God has forgotten about you, especially when loved ones and friends are getting married and you're still waiting in your single season, but rest assured, God desires to bless and prosper you. Trust His divine timeline for your life.

God's Appointed Time

PRAYER

Lord, thank you for your divine timing over my life. I'm grateful that life unfolds in seasons, each bringing growth and renewal. Grant me patience in my waiting season. May your purpose guide my journey, and fill me with hope and faith as I trust in you in Jesus' name, I pray Amen.

DAY 24

Don't Be Fearful

PSALM 23:4 (NIV)
Even though I walk through the darkest valley I will fear no evil, for you are with me, your rod and staff comfort me.

As you walk through your single season, please know that God is always with you, providing comfort and protection. There is no need to fear because you are a beloved daughter of the Most High.

Don't Be Fearful

<u>PRAYER</u>

Lord, I'm grateful that you are my shepherd, guiding and directing me through life's Valleys. Thank you Father that I do not have to fear evil, for you are always with me. Amen.

DAY 25

Wait For The One God has For You

JAMES 1:17 (NIV)
Every good and perfect gift is from above, coming down from the Father of the heavenly lights, who does not change like shifting shadow.

Wait for God's best, a husband tailored to your heart, a good and perfect blessing From your Heavenly Father.

Wait For The One God has For You

PRAYER

Heavenly Father, I thank you for being the Source of every good and perfect gift. Open my eyes so that I don't miss what you have for me in Jesus' name, I pray Amen.

DAY 26

Faith Walk

2 Corinthians 5:7 (ESV)
For we walk by faith, not by sight.

Walking by faith requires trusting God's word and guidance, even when the path is unclear.

PRAYER

Lord, I ask that you increase my faith, order my steps according to your word, open my spiritual eyes so that I can see your guidance, and bless me to trust in your promises in Jesus' name, I pray Amen.

DAY 27

You Are The Favor!

PROVERBS 18:22 (NIV)
He who finds a wife finds a good thing and obtains favor from the Lord.

God's word says that finding a wife is a blessing and a sign of God's Favor. Pray for God's alignment to increase your visibility. Trust in His provision for your ordained spouse to find you.

PRAYER

Heavenly Father, I ask that you navigate my God ordained spouse's steps, aligning our hearts with Your word, uniting us in Your perfect timing, fill our union with love, favor and blessings in Jesus' name I pray, Amen.

DAY 28

Double The Joy!

ISAIAH 61:7 (NIV)
Instead of your shame, you will receive a double portion, and instead of disgrace, you will rejoice in your inheritance. And so you will inherit a double portion in your land, and everlasting joy will be yours.

You serve a God of restoration. Remember, patience is a virtue. Trust His purpose and see your journey flourish with double the blessings right in front of those who thought you'd been overlooked.

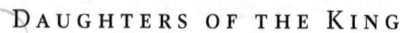

PRAYER

Heavenly Father, I thank you that shame is not my portion. I thank you that I will receive abundantly what you have for me. I ask that you fill me with everlasting joy that only comes from you in Jesus' name, I pray Amen.

DAY 29

Don't Miss God!

PROVERBS 19:21 (NIV)
Many are the plans in a person's heart, but it's the Lord's purpose that prevails.

You have preferences for your ideal kingdom spouse, such as height, age, or profession. However, God's purpose may differ from your expectations. You must decide whether to follow your desires or God's plan.

PRAYER

Lord, teach me your ways and help me discern your path for my life. I surrender my desires and preferences to you. Father, may your plans, not mine, be fulfilled in Jesus' name I pray, Amen.

DAY 30

God's Plans Are Beyond Human Comprehension

1 CORINTHIANS 2:9 (NIV)
However, as it is written: What no eye has seen, what no ear has heard, and what no human mind has conceived, the things God has prepared for those who love him.

Your current situation is not your final destination. Always remember that the best is yet to come. TRUST GOD!

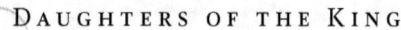

PRAYER

Lord, I thank you that your love brings hope and peace and your word reminds me that this season is just a transition to something greater. Your plans are good and I trust them in Jesus' name, I pray Amen.

About The Author

KYLE STATEMAN IS A woman of God, prophetess, empowering teacher, and passionate intercessor, serving God's people with a humble heart, called to uplift women from diverse backgrounds. She is a devoted mother to three handsome young adult sons and the founder of Fearfully & Wonderfully Made Women's Ministry.